799.2
Ki   Kinton, Tony
      The beginning bowhunter.

DATE DUE

MY 23'88	NO 30'92		
OC 1'86	JL 31 95		
NO 19'86	AG 14 00		
	JY 17 03		
NO 28'86	AG 14 '03		
DE 17'86	NO 18'09		
AP 15'87	DE 02'09		
NO 17 87	OC 20'09		
JA 4'88			
DE 12'88			
AG 23'9			

The Beginning Bowhunter

By

TONY KINTON

ICS BOOKS, INC.
MERRILLVILLE, INDIANA

THE BEGINNING BOWHUNTER

Printed in the U.S.A.

Sketches by Penny Rogers

Published by:
ICS Books, Inc.
1000 E. 80th Place
Merrillville, IN 46410

Distributed by:
Stackpole Books
Cameron & Kelker Streets
Harrisburg, PA 17105

Library of Congress Cataloging in Publication Data

Kinton, Tony.
    The beginning bowhunter.

    1. Hunting with bow and arrow. I. Title.
SK36.K56 1985   799.2'028'5   85-14343
ISBN 0-934802-21-1

Table of Contents

PART I

Bowhunting

Chapter 1

PAST

Hunting with the bow and arrow goes back in history perhaps 50,000 years. Primitive cultures used the bow and arrow as a means of self-preservation—as a weapon of war, and for subsistence hunting.

As a sport, archery drew a tremendous amount of attention even as early as the sixteenth century. Contests were quite popular, particularly in England. The nobility as well as common citizenry participated. The sport became organized in the United States in 1828 with the founding of the United Bowmen of Philadelphia.

In general, archery is practiced in two forms: target archery and field archery. It is in this second category that bowhunting falls. The target archer shoots a specified number of arrows at known distances. The field archer shoots at different sized targets at varying distances. This type practice is most valuable for the prospective bowhunter.

The bowhunter may choose to acquire the equipment and become involved in target archery. Certainly this would be beneficial to his shooting skills. He may take up organized field archery. This is a bit more attuned to bowhunting and offers the added advantage of camaraderie. Or he may simply opt for shooting practice that relates more specifically to bowhunting. This should be done even if the bowhunter is involved in other aspects of archery.

Whichever route—or combination—he chooses, the new bowhunter is embarking upon an activity like no other. Bowhunting is a totally captivating pastime.

Chapter 2

FUTURE

Predicting the future is, at best, risky. We don't know what is to come, and this is true of the sport of bowhunting. However, things look bright.

Proper management of herds has given the average hunter as much or more game than has been available to him in years. The restocking and restoration of the white-tailed deer and wild turkey is a case in point. These critters are flourishing and filling available habitat at an amazing rate. Well-trained biologists, colleges and universities, aggressive state Game and Fish agencies, and concerned sportsmen are to be commended for the solid game populations we now enjoy.

Management, however, is not something that can be practiced today and overlooked tomorrow. The whitetail, in particular, must be managed closely to assure a healthy, high-quality herd. Untold studies have gone into this, and other studies continue. The more knowledge that is gained, the more accurately biologists can make management recommendations.

While it is only a part of any overall management program, antlerless harvest is important to a well balanced deer herd. And this should be to the beginning bowhunter's delight. Legal doe harvest will, or should provide the beginner with more opportunities to take a deer. But make no mistake about it, no deer is easily taken with bow and arrow. Even when hunting antlerless deer, a great deal of skill and savvy will be required to put venison in the freezer.

Habitat and its proper management will remain a most important issue in the future. The loss and/or misuse of such could do far more damage to game than any other factor involved. Those who have a knowledge of and concern for wildlife must constantly be on guard to see that progress and conservation complement each other.

Habitat acquisition could become increasingly more important in the years ahead. This may be done on the state or national level. Corporations could and have become involved in such projects. And it is not out of the question for concerned sportsmen's groups to acquire and protect wildlife habitat. In my home state of Mississippi, I know of one group of hunters who pooled resources and purchased the property on which their hunting lease was located. This move was a bit expensive, but it assured a retention of the habitat and gave the group complete control over it so that thorough wildlife management could be implemented.

Hunting, and bowhunting in particular, has come under a great deal of opposition in recent years. Those primarily responsible for this open opposition are the ones who are opposed to hunting and would like to see it stopped. There is a much larger group out there with no firm opinion either way regarding hunting. This neutral segment of the population is the one that could determine hunting's future should the issue ever come to a vote. In situations such as this, the hunter could be his own worst enemy.

The ethical, courteous, and concerned sportsman can exhibit a wholesome picture of this beloved tradition of hunting and in so doing, win the understanding and support of the person with no opinion regarding hunting. The opposite can just as easily be the case if the hunter acts in a selfish, unethical, and unsportsmanlike manner. The hunter who asks permission to hunt private property stands a reasonable chance of gaining such. The hunter who trespasses and abuses property will make an enemy not only of himself, but of hunting and hunters in general.

It is, in my opinion, possible for the hunter to be too visible. If his conversation, dress, or manner is objectionable and ill-suited for the situation, he may be too visible. Not everyone wants to hear about the hunt, and least of all the kill. When a hunter displays an animal and parades around for all to see, that hunter just may be too visible. Discretion must be used at all times. The future could depend upon it.

Hunter ethics must be paramount in the minds of hunters in the future. Indeed, ethics could well determine whether or not there will be a future.

PART II

Why Bowhunting

Chapter 3

WHY BOWHUNTING

Words such as thrilling, challenging, exciting, and rewarding are commonly used when a hunter attempts to explain why he takes to the woods with bow and arrow after such an elusive creature as the whitetail. And these are accurate, howbeit inadequate, descriptions.

Then there are those who say they bowhunt to extend the deer season a bit. This, too, is sound reasoning. But I think that the greatest justification for and most powerful attraction to bowhunting is that it forces the participant to become a student of the game he pursues. All other things are bonuses.

Countless sportsmen will attest to the fact that they became hunters — perhaps after many years of hunting by other means — when they became bowhunters. Through the disciplinied course of in-field study required to take a deer with the bow and arrow, these sportsmen acquired a knowledge of and acquaintance with the whitetail that few non-bowhunters possess. The hunt becomes a true, one-on-one experience.

Other pleasantries associated with bowhunting are solitude and breathtakingly beautiful surroundings. The sport is one of quiet and stealth. Even if the bowhunter finds himself in the woods with others of his kind — and this is far less likely to happen than during firearms seasons — he can expect relative calm. The very nature of bowhunting demands such.

Most bow seasons open in early fall. This is a beautiful and fascinating time to be out. The aspens, oaks, maples, hickories, and many other trees put on a spectacular color-show. There is a tremendous amount of romance and intrigue in watching an autumn leaf let go from high atop a tall gum and float softly downward to the forest floor.

The reasons for and advantages of bowhunting are many. It is a hunting experience like no other. Among all the flowery adjectives and philosophical reasons we give as to why we bowhunt, let's not leave out one very important aspect — it is fun!

PART III

Basic Equipment

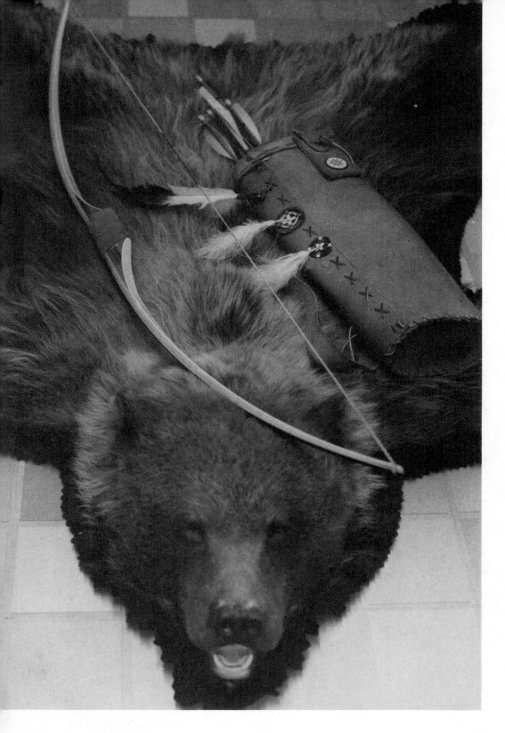

While not as popular as the recurve or compound, the longbow is highly efficient as a hunting tool. This graceful bow was built by John Schultz.

Chapter 4

BOWS

TYPES AND STYLES

Three basic types of bows are in use today: longbows, recurves, and compounds. The crossbow is also popular with some, but it is not legal for hunting in many areas.

The longbow is what the name implies — a long, straight bow with a handle in the middle. The history of this bow is not completely known, but certainly its development and use dates back hundreds of years. The English longbow was a vital tool in the Hundred Years' War (1337 - 1453).

Today, the longbow remains a viable hunting tool. However, its use is somewhat limited. The bowhunter most likely to be found in the field with a longbow is one who takes a purist approach to his sport. Perhaps nostalgia enters into his selection. And if his choice is the longbow, he is adequately equipped to hunt deer. I must admit that this sort of guy possesses a certain mystique, and generally commands due respect.

For many years the recurve was state-of-the-art for bowhunters. These graceful bows are usually shorter than long-

The recurve differs from the longbow in that it has recurved tips.

bows, consequently easier to handle in the woods. The recurve is a thing of beauty.

The recurve gets its name from the recurved tips. These bend back away from the shooter in the opposite direction of the curve that begins just above and below the handle. This recurved tip as well as the middle portion of the limb flexes, thus adding life throughout the limb.

Until the late 1960's, the recurve was the foremost hunting tool among bowhunters. At about that time, the compound began to gain a strong following, and the recurve's appeal dwindled. Today, however, there appears to be a resurgence in the use of recurves. Among most of the established archery companies, there is a line of recurve bows. Additionally, some truly outstanding recurves are being built by talented craftsmen who specialize in this work. Such bows fetch a handsome price, and most bow makers are booked up far into the future.

One style of recurve that should be of particular interest to the bowhunter who travels quite a bit, or one who prefers to reduce his bowhunting gear to a neat package and store it out of the way, is the take-down bow. This unit has been perfected over the years, and should provide a lifetime of trouble-free service.

The limbs of a take-down bow separate from the handle. When disassembled, a take-down is in three pieces. These can fit into a surprisingly small space, and this makes traveling with your bow a relatively simple affair.

Whether the choice is a standard or take-down recurve, a factory or custom-built rig, the recurve bow is an excellent piece of bowhunting equipment.

That strange-looking contraption with the wheels and cables is a compound. And it is wonderful! Certainly a drastic deviation from the norm, the compound works on a principle of pullies which gives a relaxed or let-off effect when the bow reaches full draw. This is a definite advantage.

The amount of let-off built into a bow will vary, but some companies use a system that relaxes as much as fifty percent.

With its cables and pullies, the compound is a marvelous invention. This Martin Lynx Magnum is a good example of a split-limb, two-wheel bow — excellent for the bowhunter.

Twenty to thirty percent is perhaps more common.

Unlike the longbow or recurve, the compound offers its highest resistance to the shooter at the beginning of the draw. This is the point at which the shooter is likely to be his strongest. As the draw progresses, the wheels at the end of the limbs "flip over" on an off-centered axle, and the draw relaxes requiring considerably less strength to hold the bow at the relaxed, full draw. This is particularly advantageous when you have drawn on a buck and he suddenly steps behind a bush. The draw can be held momentarily in hopes of a clear shot.

Another advantage of most compounds, although this feature is not available on some models, is the inherent adjustment of draw weight. There is usually a 15-pound weight span through which the bow can be set. This allows the shooter to begin on the lower side and progress upward if the need arises. However, he must tune the bow, match the arrows to, and practice at the draw weight he plants to use for hunting if results are to be consistent.

A variation on the standard round-wheel compound is the cam bow. This system, which is relatively new, features an oval type wheel rather than round wheel at its limb's ends. This system is somewhat faster than the round-wheel, but doesn't feature quite the let-off. The choice between the two is a matter of preference.

Compound bows come in a wide variety of styles, all functioning on the same basic principle. Common among the configurations to be found are the two-wheel models; multi-wheel models; split limb bows on which the wheels at the ends of the limbs are mounted in a "V" split built into the limb ; and bracket models which have the wheels at the ends of the limbs mounted in a bracket or housing that is attached to the limb. There are even compound bows that look like a recurve on one end, but have a wheel and compound system on the other.

Selecting a compound is a matter of taste and preference. All these rigs function in fine fashion, and all are quite marvelous inventions. Surely a drastic departure from the recurve or longbow, the compound will probably lead the future.

MAKING THE RIGHT CHOICE

The first decision that a prospective bowhunter must make regarding bows is which basic type bow he will choose to begin this fascinating pastime. All three — longbow, recurve, compound — are capable of giving years of service, and performing well on game.

A proper beginning should start at a shop staffed by knowledgeable personnel with bowhunting experience. These people can help advise you regarding equipment, and should have the knowledge to correctly match the bow to related accessories as well as the shooter.

Physical makeup will be an all-important factor governing equipment selection. If the bow is too long or otherwise out of proportion for the shooter, the results will be less than desirable. Quite naturally, the shooter's hand/eye preference — left or right — must be taken into consideration. And consideration must be given to any physical handicap the shooter might have.

Draw weight is always a question that new shooters have. For bowhunting, the best answer is to shoot all the draw weight you can handle. It would be practically impossible to have too much weight — as long as you can handle it in all situations — but it is certainly possible to have too little.

A minimum of forty-five pounds should probably be considered as the bottom side of draw weight for the bowhunter. Now this is not an absolute, but a reasonable guideline. My compound is set at sixty pounds for deer hunting, and I get complete penetration on most shots. This is to my liking. If the shooter can't handle an adequate draw weight, it is probably best for him to pass on bowhunting until he works up to that

A fully equipped compound is a solid choice for the new bowhunter.

targeted weight. However, most shooters of average build and strength can quickly become accustomed to a draw weight that is suitable for hunting.

I am often asked what type bow I would recommend for the beginning bowhunter. Well, at the risk of alienating some of my peers, several archery shops, and a few bow manufacturers, I will give that same recommendation here. For I truly believe it to be the best choice for one new to bowhunting.

The beginner should start out with a simple, basic compound in the two-wheel, split-limb configuration. This bow should be the right length for the shooter, and should feel good in his hands. It should be set at a draw weight the shooter can handle, as long as this weight is adequate. The draw length must also be properly set. To the beginner's bow should be added a sturdy arrow rest, rugged and reliable sights, string silencers, probably a cable guard, and a quiet bow quiver.

There you have it. I feel that this is the best possible choice for the beginning bowhunter. In fact, after more years afield that I care to remember, such a rig is the one I use most today. It is highly functional and a fine performer.

Chapter 5

BROADHEADS AND ARROWS

THE PROPER EDGE

The broadhead could easily be the single most important ingredient in the bowhunter's gear. A strong, sharp broadhead adequately delivered to a vital spot — no matter what type bow cast the arrow/broadhead — will put the animal down cleanly. Conversely, an ill-prepared, poorly selected broadhead launched from a super-sizzling compound could leave the bowhunter with a long tracking job, or worst of all, a lost or wasted game animal.

One oft-heard and much overlooked prescription for maintaining an effective broadhead is, "keep it sharp." And that is not just sharp, but razor, shaving sharp. This is a must, and why it is so neglected remains a mystery.

There are two basic types of broadheads: the fixed edge, you-sharpen broadhead; and the pre-sharpened, replaceable blade models. Both systems are fine, and both contain some outstanding selections.

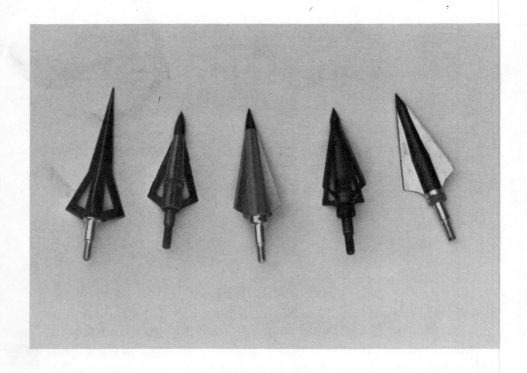

Broadhead styles and types differ. There are the replaceable blade models and those with fixed, you-sharpen-it blades. Whichever type you choose, keep it shaving sharp.

Strength is a major consideration in selecting a broad-head. No matter the style head you choose, it should be strong, and able to withstand the rigors of penetrating the deer — perhaps even relatively heavy bone — without bend-ing or breaking. A curled tip on a broadhead will greatly impede forward progress.

Generally speaking, the majority of the fixed-blade heads are strong. Several have been around for years, and when properly sharpened, have proven their effectiveness on game. However, these must be sharpened to a fine edge. The Bear Razorhead is a classic example of the fixed-edge broadhead.

One head that has been getting some good press recently is the Snuffer developed by Roger Rothhaar. This is a big broadhead, and results from its use are positive. Another fixed edge head, which is quite new at this writing is a two-blade rig developed by Calvin Montgomery of Calmount Archery, Inver-ness, Mississippi. The heads come packed with a sharpeneing stone, and the proper angle for producing a fine edge is gov-erned by the center section of the head. Just lay the broadhead flat on the stone and sharpen away. It looks like a fine idea.

The pre-sharpened, insert system seems to get the nod from the majority of bowhunteres today. This is not without reason, for the array of broadheads available is mind boggling, and most offer strong, surgeon-sharp blades which are easily replaced. Also, these come in varying weights and number of blades.

One thing to look for in the replaceable blade category is blade thickness. A reasonable range around which to stay is .020 inch. I have taken whitetail and mule deer with blades that were .015 and .017 inch thick, but a bit heavier is probably a better choice. The heads I now use—the Thunderhead 125—carry a stainless steel insert that is .027 inch thick.

Whatever type, style, or size broadhead you choose, you must be sure to tune your bow to shoot that particular rig. Seldom will a broadhead fly identical to a field point, and it is a drastic mistake to assume such. The only way to perfect your broadhead shooting is to shoot the broadhead you choose. My suggestion would be to try several that fit the requirements before you settle on a broadhead. Some just seem to perform better or tune more easily in a given bow than others. Your archery dealer should be able to help you make a wise choice in this area.

MATCH SHAFT TO SET-UP

That vital link between the bow and broadhead is the arrow shaft. Thought and judgment must be put into this selection.

Materials such as cedar, fiberglass, aluminum, and graphite are commonly used for making arrow shafts. Your choice of bow will be somewhat of a determining factor regarding arrow material. Without question, aluminum is preferred by most recurve and compound users today.

Selecting arrow shafts is not as simple as strolling into a discount store and scooping up a handful. Even though this is done on a regular basis, it is a haphazard, risky approach.

Shaft selection is primarily governed by four factors: type bow, draw weight, draw length, and the type tip to be used. In the case of bowhunting, the tip will be a broadhead. The spine, or stiffness, of the shaft should be determined by these criteria. If an arrow doesn't have enough spine for the set-up, there will be too much flex, and accuracy will suffer.

Draw length, which is also a vital factor in determining spine, has another important application. The arrow should be just the right length for the broadhead to clear the arrow rest when the bowhunter is at full draw. A too-short arrow would cause the archer to stop short of his full and comfortable draw, or it would hang the rest and probably fall off if he continued

A positive aspect of the replaceable blade broadhead is the ability to have a razor edge simply by inserting pre-sharpened blades. Here a hunter changes blades in the field after failing to score with the arrow.

Proper measurements are vital to proper shooting. Here, a dealer measures a shooter to determine the right draw length and arrow length before equipping the hunter.

his draw. This is a dangerous situation.

On the other hand, an arrow that is much too long is unnecessary. It adds unwanted weight to the shaft, and unneeded inches to a quiver full of arrows that already seem too long.

A competent dealer can be of tremendous help in this area. He will check the draw weight of your bow, and measure the length when you are at full draw. Through his knowledge and charts, he can make a recommendation regarding shaft selection. If need be, he can cut and custom-fit shafts for you. Make that little extra investment in this stage of equipping and preparing.

PART IV

Accessories

Ladder stands are convenient and easily climbed.

Chapter 6

TREESTANDS

TYPES AND STYLES

Never before has the hunter had such an array of tree stands from which to choose. And, in my opinion, the new bowhunter should consider a comfortable, safe, and functional tree stand as a part of his "must-have" accessories. At best, hunting the whitetail deer with bow and arrow is difficult; but to hunt solely from the ground further complicates the situation. Now, that is not to say that it can't be done. Indeed, it can, and is. But a tree stand is a bit more effective, especially for the beginner.

Let's preface any further discussion with some advice about laws. Check the rules governing tree stand use in the state, province, or particular area you plan to hunt. Many decisions regarding tree stands may have already been made for you. Also, we'll not go into the construction and use of permanent stands. This is not an option open to many bowhunters.

Practically any type and style of portable tree stand one

Tree stands are most helpful to the bowhunter. This hunter is using a basic self-climber.

The stand-up/sit-down process makes climbing a simple matter. This all-metal self-climber made and marketed by Amacker Products is a good example of this system. There are many stands on the market that use this same process.

*Buckle-on stands are particularly useful as a semi-permanent
station. Once set up and locked on the tree, very little climbing
effort is required. With these and all other stands, wear a safety belt.
Ladder stands are convenient and easily climbed.*

could want is available today. There are ladder stands, self-climbers, buckle-on stands, small platforms that fit into the crotch of a tree, and tree slings of varying configurations. All have practical applications, and one is sure to meet your needs.

In choosing a stand, as in picking a bow, your over-all physical characteristics should be considered. The in-shape, agile bowhunter can handle them all. A hunter who finds himself facing a different set of circumstances may need to be a bit more selective.

Perhaps the very easiest stand to use is the ladder stand. Most of these are simply carried into the woods, leaned against a tree, and climbed. This is quick, and can be accomplished by most hunters. The disadvantage, however, is bulk, and the inability to get very high. We will discuss this a bit later, but I feel that height is very important in the proper, effective use of tree stands for the bowhunter. It is far less important for the rifleman with his long-range capabilities. If the archer locates a ladder stand in the fifteen to eighteen-feet-high category, this could be a most useful set-up.

The self-climbers probably dominate the market. There are several manufacturers offering such stands, and all work off the same basic principle. There is a platform on which the hunter stands. This unit has braces which extend backward to the off-side of the tree. On that off-side, a bar is attached to the braces and the stand is locked to the tree. Upward or downward progress is made by lifting the stand via straps or a bar that goes over the hunter's feet. This changes the angle of the stand, releases it from the tree, and allows the hunter to move the stand. When he puts his weight back down on the platform, the angle is such that the stand locks back on the tree.

This is the basic concept of all self-climbers, but even among these there is variation and additional equipment. In its simplest form, the self-climbing stand is moved up and down the tree by the hunter hugging the tree so that he may lift his feet and adjust the stand. For the strong and agile this is fine. However, it can scuff up the ole tummy and chest, especially in warm weather hunting situations when the archer is likely to be dressed in a light shirt. Hand climbers, which operate in identical fashion to the platform, are a welcome addition to most bowhunters.

These climbers work in conjunction with the platform, and give the hunter something to hang onto while he hoists himself up the tree. Many of these can double as a seat when the bowhunter gets himself positioned. The additional weight that handclimbers add is offset by their usefulness.

Another variation is the stand-up/sit-down self-climber. Still operating on the same premise as all self-climbers, these rigs are in two pieces — the seat and platform. The hunter faces the tree in the seat (upper unit) and lifts his feet to raise the platform. He then stands up and raises the seat on which he sits and raises the platform. This moves the hunter up the tree with a moderate amount of physical exertion. This unit is my preference, and I use it religiously.

Requiring more agility are the various buckle-on stands. These are great, but demand that the hunter be able to climb the tree. Buckle-on or screw-in steps, where legal, could help solve the climbing problem. A plus for this type stand is that the tree doesn't have to be a straight, limbless-trunked specimen for the stand to perform. Exacting tree specifications are a drawback for self-climbers.

Tree slings are interesting gadgets. These are made of material similar to automobile seat belts, and offer the ultimate in compactness and portability. There is at least one set-up which includes a lightweight hoist system that allows the hunter to anchor it and pull himself into the tree. Other units require the nimrod to climb, then attach the sling to the tree.

The type tree stand you choose will be largely a matter of preference. Select one that you can maneuver with ease, one that is quiet, and one that is strong and secure. And wear a safety belt. Do not climb without one. Senseless accidents could be avoided by the simple use of a safety belt.

USE

Bowhunters use tree stands for several reasons. Getting above the deer's normal line of sight, getting that noxious human scent above and away from super-sensitive nostrils, and increasing the hunter's visibility are among the major reasons for using tree stands.

By its very nature, bowhunting is a short-ranged affair. The hunter must be quite near his quarry for positive results. My personal outside limit is 30 yards. If the deer is past that, I wait and try him tomorrow. Tree stands are a definite plus in such close encounters.

If the bowhunter has done his homework, he will know specific travel routes of the deer he will hunt. Along such well-used routes is where he should place his stand. The distance from trail to stand will best be determined by surrounding conditions such as cover, but ten to twenty yards is usually ideal. This will allow the hunter a few yards up or down the trail from his stand and still be within the bow's effective range.

With the necessity of being so close, it is easy to see how difficult it would be to do from ground level. If the hunter is elevated above his game's normal line of sight, the chances of being detected are fewer. The same applies for scent. If the hunter is above the deer, it is less likely that the animal will get a whiff of homo sapien, whereupon the critter will promptly head for the next county. Tree stands are a partial answer.

Try to get above some natural cover with your tree stand. This Baker Slim Jim helped this hunter situate so that he is practically invisible from below.

I am sure that there are those who would disagree, and I have no scientific findings on which to base my case, but I firmly believe — from years of bowhunting the whitetail — that deer are becoming savvy to tree stands and the hunters these rigs contain. This is the reason I mentioned earlier the importance of height.

At one time, it seemed that twelve feet was ample height from which to ambush a deer. And though this can be done today, in heavily hunted areas it is far less likely than in years past. The deer appear to be adapting to the "high-up" hunter, and are not nearly so nonchalant toward that strange protrusion dangling from the timber. For this reason, it is vital to go unseen. Height and cover are the answer.

After deciding upon a trail to watch, the hunter should spend time in selecting a stand site. Look for a climbable tree that is within range of the trail, and one with some natural camouflage around. I like to climb a tree — fifteen to eighteen feet high is my choice — that has smaller trees and bushes around it. By getting above such cover, I am somewhat concealed from a ground view. I take care, however, to see that none of the protective limbs and tree/bush tops hinder my shooting. This type set-up has proven effective many, many times, and I shall continue to use it.

Visibility is greatly improved from an elevated platform. And though a deer may well be out of range when visible from a tree stand, the hunter knows that animal is there and can follow its progress. Additionally, the hunter is better able to see down into thickets and tangles from his stand. It is from such spots that a deer is likely to emerge.

Tree stands are advantageous to the bowhunter. Indeed, some sort of elevated platform is a must. Use these, but remember those safety belts.

Chapter 7

SIGHTS

Sights — and this includes a string peep or kisser button for a consistent anchor point — are a vital part of the modern bowhunter's gear. This is especially true of the individual who has chosen to equip himself with a compound. Some type of reliable sighting system should be included. First, let's look at string peeps/kisser buttons and see how and why these are used.

The string peep is simply what the name implies — a peep, much like the aperture sight on a rifle, that goes in the bow string. When the archer is at full draw, the peep is drawn up near the eye so that the shooter looks through the tiny hole. This serves the purpose of requiring the bowhunter to anchor in the same place each time he draws. If he fails to do so, he will be unable to see through the peep.

A kisser button has much the same application; however, the shooter does not look through this item. The kisser button

A string peep is a big assist to accurate shooting. Use it much as you would an aperture sight on a rifle.

is drawn to the corner of the mouth or a certain spot on the cheek each time the archer shoots. With practice, this gives the bowhunter a reference which tells him that his draw is complete, and that he is properly anchored.

*The kisser button works in much the same way as a string peep. It
gives a firm point of reference for a consistent anchor.*

    While there are many variations, and even some sighting
systems that are not related to either category, most bow
sights for hunting fall into one of two groups: pin sights or
pendulum sights. We'll look at each separately.

PIN SIGHTS

By far, the most popular bowhunting sight is the pin sight. This system consists of a series of pins — usually four — positioned along a slotted bar which is mounted to the bow. The pins have windage and elevation adjustment, and are set, by the shooter, to put the arrow at point-of-aim at predetermined distances. Twenty, thirty, forty, and fifty yards are perhaps the distances most often chosen for these four settings.

For the sight pin to perform at its optimum, the bowhunter must accurately judge the distance to his target and choose the appropriate pin. If the shooter has his first two pins set up to hit at twenty and thirty yards respectively, and he finds himself looking at a deer which is at the 25-yard mark, a proper conclusion would be to use the twenty-yard pin and hold a bit high. This should put the arrow in the boiler room. Adequate practice makes this system highly functional and amazingly accurate.

PENDULUM SIGHTS

Operating on a totally different concept is the pendulum sight. There are several varieties on the market today — some rather rough, others quite refined — but all work off the same principle. These are hinged rigs that pivot as the bow is tilted to make a downward shot. Angle and gravity combine to give the proper setting, thus eliminating the need for the bowhunter to estimate range.

Pendulum sights come with detailed instructions regarding their mounting and setting. This must be done properly if the sight is to perform as it should.

In theory, the pendulum sight is the answer for the bowhunter who will be shooting from an elevated position. All he

Pin sights are amazingly accurate. Judge the distance, choose the appropriate pin, and put the pin on the spot. A smooth release should put the arrow on target.

Pendulum sights, such as this Eliminator, are reported to give good accuracy from an elevated stand. Angle and gravity combine to judge the distance for the shooter.

must do is aim and shoot — distance judging is done for him quickly by the pivoting action of the sight. From all indications, these units have reached a high state of perfection, particularly among the more refined, expensive versions. Range estimation/accuracy is reported to be outstanding out to thirty yards or so, and this is as far as I care to shoot.

A bow quiver is a handy unit for hunting. It helps keep gear consolidated into one neat package.

Chapter 8

QUIVERS

The quiver is the arrow carrier. Its purpose is to transport quietly, safely, and securely enough arrows for a hunt. These have taken many forms throughout the years, but have reached a point of refinement in the modern bow quiver.

BOW QUIVERS

Bow quivers mount on the bow and store several arrows in easy reach of the shooter. Arrows are clipped firmly into place, and the sharp broadheads go inside a protective hood where they are kept from bumping into each other, and shielded from the hunter and others around. If the quiver is not so designed, don't use it.

A good bow quiver mount holds the quiver securely to the bow, but allows for quick detachment for storage or transport. Many bowhunters opt to remove the quiver from the bow after getting situated in the tree stand. The quiver can then be attached to the tree or stand in a position that will keep it handy for the shooter.

Another plus of a high quality, properly installed bow quiver is its easy removal. Some hunters prefer to take the quiver off the bow and lay it aside after they are set up.

A well designed, properly mounted bow quiver is a wise choice for the modern bowhunter. It gives him several arrows at his fingertips; transports arrows quietly and securely; and helps consolidate equipment into one neat package. This will be much appreciated when moving through the woods and/or climbing into and out of tree stands. By the way, get settled in your stand, then pull your bow up on a string. Let it down before you descend.

BACK AND HIP QUIVERS

Seen primarily in target archery use, the back and hip quivers have largely been replaced by the bow quiver for most hunting purposes today. One exception to this is the individual who chooses to go the more traditional route — the longbow shooter, for instance.

Back quivers are carried on the back, and are attached by a strap or series of straps. On most versions, the fletched end of the arrow is up. Depending upon the arrangements, arrows either fit into clips and slots, or are left loose in the quiver.

Hip quivers are similar. There are tube-type quivers in which the arrows are placed freely, and there are clip versions which hold arrows securely, usually in a fan position.

As previously mentioned, back or hip quivers are seldom seen being used by bowhunters today. For the compound or recurve shooter, such rigs are usually replaced by sturdy bow quivers. However, for the archer who prefers a back or hip quiver, a version that clips individual arrows so that these are held securely is a viable alternative.

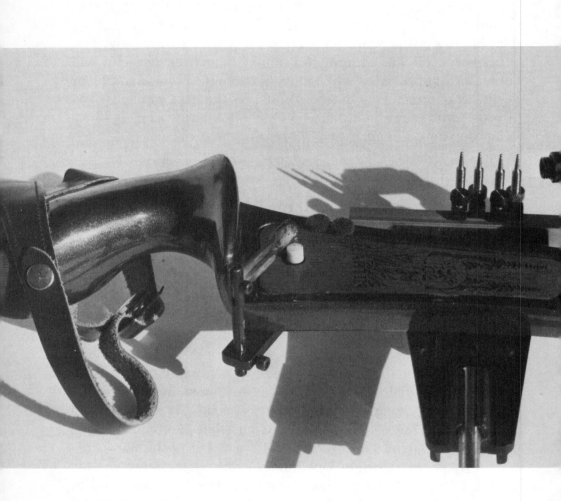

The arrow rest used for hunting must be strong and quiet.

Chapter 9

RELEASE AIDS

The release is paramount to accuracy when shooting a bow. This process should be smooth, and should allow the arrow to slip from the shooter's hand and bow with no added motion. It is not an easily perfected step in shooting.

Whether they should be recommended for hunting is a source of debate, but there are countless release aids that help to assure that smooth, motion-free release so vital for good accuracy. These are quite common in tournament shooting.

Even though I used a simple release aid for several years of hunting, I have since given this up, and feel that it is best for the bowhunter to perfect his style without the help of one of these gadgets. The rig I used was a small "T"-shaped device with a thumb-activitated trigger. It worked well, and I took many deer while using the release aid. But, it was somewhat in the way, and a constant source of concern.

There are so many release aids on the market today that I would not attempt to cover them all here. Basically, all these units hold the bow string via a small metal bar or rope. The string is drawn by holding onto and pulling the release aid; the

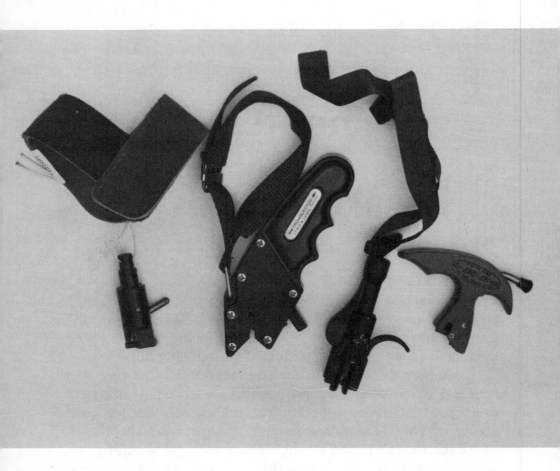

Release aids vary, but all are designed to do just what the name implies — aid in the release. While these perform beautifully, it is probably best for the bowhunter to use his fingers rather than an aid. However, this is primarily a matter of preference.

string is released by depressing a trigger built into the system. In general, these things are not bad. In fact, such a set-up can assist in good shooting. However, if the bowhunter can do without such, it is best left off.

And while it is certainly not a release aid, there is one small piece of necessary equipment that can help in proper shooting and arrow flight. This is the arrow rest, and a pro-shop should be able to help you choose wisely.

You will want a quiet hunting rest. This is a strong system and one that is geared to a hunting set-up. One part of that total rest system that I choose to use is the spring-loaded plunger button. This rig is a tool of "forgiveness," and helps to smooth out and somewhat cover up a less than perfect release — which can be quite common in a hunting situation.

PART V

Practice

Practice is essential. These young bowhunters line up for a round at a target stationed in the brush.

Chapter 10

TARGET SHOOTING

The bowhunter can never get enough practice. Even when he reaches that point of proficiency where he can consistently deliver an arrow to a given point, he must practice to maintain that skill. Practice should become an ongoing and enjoyable aspect of preparation for bowhunting.

Target shooting is important to the bowhunter, especially in his early stages of learning and equipment preparation. Such shooting allows the bowhunter to develop his form, hone his skills, and regulate equipment under controlled conditions. It is vital to shoot at known distances when setting up sight pins on your hunting bow.

Unless the bowhunter intends to pursue target archery as an addition to his bowhunting, shooting under such controlled conditions becomes far less important after the initial learning experience and equipment adjustments. Practice that is more pertinent to hunting should become the goal of the bowhunter at this point. I call this field or "stump" shooting.

Shooting practice arrows from a tree stand is another vital aspect of proper preparation.

Chapter 11

FIELD
"STUMP" SHOOTING

This type practice finds the bowhunter roaming the woods and fields while shooting at incidental targets that come his way. These may include a leaf he has singled out on the ground ahead; a particular spot of sunlight striking an adjacent ridge; or a tuft of grass that catches the shooter's eye. Also included should be animal targets scattered around at unknown distances. And some of this shooting must take place from a tree stand.

It is important for the bowhunter — particularly while he is shooting from his tree stand — to try shots at difficult angles and from awkward positions. These seem to be the norm when hunting the fascinating whitetail. If you are serious about bowhunting, you must exercise the discipline to practice under such handicaps.

An excellent form of practice, and one that helps the archer equip himself for the hunt, is silhouette shooting. This is shooting at animal-sized targets, and the added thrill of watching the target topple when the arrow smacks it solidly is a definite plus. In its competitive form, silhouette shooting is

Silhouette shooting is not only fun, it is good practice. Seeing the target topple with a solid hit is an added bonus.

quite regimented; however, I much prefer to set the targets up in the woods and try them from different angles and distances. This is great sport and practice for a group of bowhunters, and that group may choose to pool resources and purchase a set of regulation silhouettes for some serious bowhunting practice.

PART VI

Scouting

Chapter 12

WHY

The bowhunter, perhaps more than any other hunter, must scout. He must scout not only to find general areas being frequented by deer, but specific routes that the animals are taking. His scouting could become a rather time-consuming enterprise, but without it, the hunting will suffer.

Why scout? To help assure success. Without scouting, a bowhunter condemns himself to probable failure and frustration.

Scouting is essential. Field borders are good places to begin.

Chapter 13

HOW

Scouting may take many forms; but for the hunter to get the maximum benefit from the activity, he must walk the area he plans to hunt. Where permissable, riding logging roads may steer a hunter in the right direction, but it is only a beginning. He should take what he picks up here and follow it up.

Road crossings can easily give the hunter a place to begin. From here he should trace down trails, and try to determine where the deer are likely to go. The food supply and bedding cover are the major ingredients in a deer's life throughout most of the year. Trails will usually connect the two, and following a trail from a road crossing will probably reveal one or the other. This happened to me during last year's bow season.

A road crossing was evident along one of the gravel roads running through my hunting club. Following the trail on either side of that road revealed a soybean field bordered by a honeysuckle thicket, and an impenetrable block of cover. The little road was about half-way between these two magnets. It took several days, but I arrowed a nice buck along the trail near the

Road crossings like this one may be found easily. Also, these are easily checked and can give the hunter a great deal of information regarding deer movement.

bedding area one morning. This road-crossing sign had led me to a hot spot!

Food supplies are always to be considered when scouting and hunting. Such areas will see concentrated deer activity, and are likely spots around which to hunt. Agricultural crops known to attract deer should be the first stop for the bowhunter. These will vary with the different regions of the country, but corn and soybeans, where present, are staples, and can really draw deer. Rye grass and wheat are good for winter.

A favorite method of scouting such crops is to take a stand in the late afternoon and watch for deer to filter into the fields. Several consecutive days of this could help the bowhunter get the deer activity down to an exact state. He will know when and where to expect the deer to show, and he can position his stand accordingly.

A similar approach to this scouting is to go to the fields when the deer are not there — late mornings or mid-day — and walk the edges. Trails entering the fields will be evident. After you locate a well-used trail, walk it out — at least several yards back into the woods. Such trails are likely to lead to thickets and tangles that the deer use for bedding. At times, these may be some distance from the field. In other cases, there may be enough cover bordering a field to give the deer needed security. At any rate, take care not to blunder into a deer's hiding place, particularly if you plan to hunt there that afternoon.

The advantage of following a trail back away from a field is time. Chances are, the hunter will encounter deer much earlier in the afternoon near a bedding area than he will along a field border, especially if the bedding area is far removed from the field. This is true even if the hunter is only a short distance back in the woods. Deer tend to get to the field edges with ample shooting light remaining, but mill around in the woods until darkness begins to take over. It is then that the critters are most likely to venture into the open. If you fail to scout trails back into the woods and find a stand site, you could

Follow trails from field edges. These could lead you to hot-spots back in the woods.

spend your bow season with deer nearby but no chance for a shot.

Do, however, be careful when setting up near a bedding area. If you are too close, you could spook the deer and move them in the opposite direction. How close to get to the area is somewhat of a relative matter, but certainly, don't get within sight of the spot. And be more than careful when climbing and setting up. Man noises are foreign to peaceful woods. Keep it down.

The reverse of the afternoon procedure is true for early-morning hunting. It is extremely rare to have a field-edge stand that is productive for early morning. The deer leave the fields and head back into the woods as daylight exposes them. A stand located along a trail leading from a field to a thicket could be productive if you can get to it without disturbing deer that might be in the fields and surrounding woodlots.

It is important to scout out trails. Take your time and do this thoroughly. Such activity has helped me put venison in the freezer many times.

Another productive scouting method is to walk small creeks and ditches running through your hunting area. If deer find a need to cross from side to side on a regular basis, this crossing will be most evident. Simply walk along the bank of this drainage and keep your eyes open. Some really outstanding spots can be located in this manner.

Perhaps the most difficult scouting is that done in unbroken blocks of woods. Finding sign that will lead you to concentrations of deer is not easy in many cases. Even so, if deer are there in sufficient numbers, enough hours and leg work will reveal their whereabouts.

Heavily used trails will be evident even on leaf-carpeted forest floors. These will appear as a ribbon meandering through the woods, and can usually be seen quite easily. Keep an eye out for such as you walk, but be sure that the trail is fresh before you hunt it. It could be a trail leading to a food

Buck rubs are easily spotted and give solid evidence that a buck has been in the area.

supply that is no longer available, and the deer have abandoned this trail for the remainder of the season. If this is the case, move on. Don't squander your time there.

A concentration of food could give you a beginning point from which to locate active woodland trails. Depending upon your geographic location and the time of year, such foods could include white-oak acorns, persimmons, apples, honeysuckles, or smilax. Spend some time around these.

Buck sign, at the very least, gives evidence that a buck has been in the area. And if you have found nothing else, it is a place to start.

Bucks will rub bushes in the fall to help dislodge dried, itching velvet which has covered that precious rack during its growing period. This is probably done as the buck travels a familiar trail. Therefore, rub marks on trees and bushes could help you start a trail that would lead to high deer activity. Certainly, taking a stand over old rubbing bushes is not suggested. There must be fresh, concentrated sign before the bowhunter should spend his time there.

Bucks also rub and make additional sign in the form of scrapes during the rut. This can be an absolutely superb time to be afield with bow and arrow.

Scrapes will be oval-shaped areas pawed clean of leaves and debris. Generally, these will be under an overhanging limb which is likely to be broken and twisted by the buck. When scouting, keep your eye out for this. But like all other sign, be sure that it is fresh before you put in hunting time there. We will discuss more about how to hunt scrapes in a later chapter. Knowing what to look for is the important thing at this point.

How to scout will vary from hunter to hunter and situation to situation. The methods I have discussed here have worked and continue to work beautifully for me. I'll not break from these soon. Stay out there, is the best advice I could give. And while you are out there, keep your eyes open!

Scrapes show up as the rut begins to get in full swing. Look for scrapes along ridge tops and logging roads. Most will be under a limb the buck can reach with his rack and mouth.

Chapter 14

WHEN

The obvious answer to the question of when to scout is all the time. Most successful bowhunters I know make this a year-round activity. These individuals can predict with some accuracy seasonal changes and patterns. After a year or so around a specific area, such hunters need far less time to scout because they know the more likely spots to check out at a given time and under a given set of circumstances. Don't despair. This will come to you. It simply takes time.

The necessity to scout at all times comes from the fact that deer change patterns throughout the year. Food supply, weather conditions, hunting pressure, and the rut are some of the things responsible for this periodic change. Constant scouting helps the hunter stay abreast of each change as it occurs.

Before the bowhunter hunts — and even during the hunt — he should scout. He should have deer patterned prior to his hunt, and he must stay in close contact with the situation to detect changes. As sign becomes old and is not regularly freshened, it is necessary for the bowhunter to put in some more hours of scouting to determine the areas being used by deer. The deer don't vanish; their habits simply change. Scout constantly to know of this change.

A more specific answer regarding when to scout is to scout when the deer are not there. In the case of deep woods and thickets this may not be possible, for deer may be in the immediate vicinity at all times. But when scouting food sources, mid to late mornings are the best times to avoid contact with deer. This is my preference, for I want my scouting to tell me where the deer are active, not to bring about an encounter and disturb the deer of the area.

I like to hunt in the early mornings, and if scouting is on the agenda, get that done with a minimum of disturbance later that morning. If I find what I am looking for, an early lunch is in order, after which I go immediately to my chosen area and set up. However, until I find a situation that is to my liking, I continue to scout, even if it means not hunting that afternoon. I feel that it is time well spent.

Chapter 15

WHERE

Around known food supplies is an obvious place to begin scouting. Such may include soybean and corn fields, garden plots, acorn flats, or honeysuckle thickets.

Logging roads are also good. Sign is usually located easily along these, and an active trail may be found running along or across a logging road. The same is true of gravel or dirt roads that wind through your hunting territory. Deer sign may be found along the shoulders of these roads, or crossings leading into adjacent woods detected. This situation is present on my Mississippi deer lease, and I can drive by at any time and check deer movement in that particular area. The deer come down a road bank, cross, and go up a bank on the opposite side. Sign is readily visible.

Scout along creeks and ditches. If deer move back and forth across these, there will be preferred crossings. By walking along a creek or ditch — especially one flowing through a block of woods — the hunter may find a veritable highway.

Logging roads are excellent for scouting. This hunter has located a trail crossing such a road and is checking for a productive-looking stand site.

Certainly the possibility of finding such is worth a pleasant walk down a creek bank.

And finally, scout wherever you happen to be. Keep an eye out for deer sign. There may be none, but the practice of looking for it is good. And who knows, you may run across an extremely productive hot-spot while en route to check out another area!

PART VII

The Hunt

Chapter 16

PROPER LOCATION AND TIMING

The hunt is the final exam of all that homework — equipment selection, practice, scouting — you have been doing. It is this endeavor that keeps us coming back from year to year.

Simply put, to be successful as a bowhunter, the archer must be at the right place at the right time. That's what the scouting is all about. If you have spent adequate time afield and have correctly patterned deer, you should have the place and time somewhat perfected; this is a giant step toward harvesting game.

The next step is to be sure you are ready — physically and mentally. The physical preparation comes with the countless hours of practice — shooting, climbing, judging distance — you have put in. Mental readiness comes by "rehearsing" a hunting situation in your mind.

See and hear that deer approach; watch that sight pin settle on a vital spot; feel the smooth draw and release; picture

Stringing a trail can help the hunter determine when deer are using a given trail. Check the strings regularly, but leave as little sign and scent as possible.

the swift, accurate flight of the arrow; experience the euphoria of success. As strange as it may seem, this is a part of the practice and preparation. It is vital. Go through an imaginary, successful hunt many times a day when preparing for the real thing.

One system that aids the hunter in determining the right place and time — and perhaps this should be included in a section on scouting — is the ''stringing'' of trails. In so doing, the hunter is able to make a solid judgment regarding active trails and times of day when movement is at a peak. To narrow times down to a block of a few hours, however, the hunter must be able to check his strings quite regularly.

After locating trails that show promise, stretch a piece of dark sewing thread across these at a height so that a deer will encounter and break the thread. For me, this distance is about half-way between my knee and waist, or approximately 26 inches. Pull the thread fairly taut and firmly anchor it to a bush on each side of the trail. Check the thread regularly and keep accurate records of your findings. However, leave as little human sign and scent as possible.

Don't go to your thread via the trail. Approach from the side and down wind. Also, get no closer than is necessary to the spot you have threaded. Unless the thread is broken and must be replaced, a visual check is all that is needed, and this should be done from as far away as you can see the thread.

I like to have active trails threaded while I watch my chosen trail during a hunting session. When I leave my stand, if feasible, I check all the threaded trails. The same is true when I return to the stand. A bit of this coupled with some record keeping helps me to get the time and place factor down so that I know what place to hunt when. It also helps eliminate spots that deer have stopped using or use only at night. This prevents wasted time spent watching an area that is far less likely to produce than is some other locale.

Perhaps the biggest asset to the bowhunter who has otherwise prepared himself adequately is perseverance. It can also be his worst enemy. If the hunter knows, from scouting, that deer are using an area during daylight hours, and knows, through practice, that he can handle his equipment, the only remaining obstacle to conquer is perseverance. Stay with it. Any experienced bowhunter can tell tales verifying the need for this. The last buck I took with my bow during the 1984 season was a case in point.

I had patterned the deer and was quite confident that I was on him. There was no doubt that the buck was there and using the area regularly, but after five vigils atop my Amaker stand, I had not seen the critter. The clock rudely jangled me awake on that sixth day; the last day of the season. The morning was cold. This would be a good time to stir the fire, drink some coffee, and work on this book in the pre-dawn quiet. Instead, I forced myself out of the house, and headed for my stand. Shortly after daylight, the buck was put down by my arrow.

Perseverance had won again. Strive toward that goal. Go, go some more, and keep on going!

Chapter 17

SCENT AND MOVEMENT

Proper tree stand location — which was covered in a preceding chapter — can help you win in the battle of scent and movement — a most critical aspect of the hunt. However, it is not a cure-all. The bowhunter must go undetected by super-sensitive noses, and his movements must not alert keen eyes that perceive motion readily. He must do more than situate a tree stand high in a tree that provides cover; although this is beneficial.

The most obvious tactic that the hunter can use to avoid being smelled is to stay downwind of the game — actually, downwind of the trail is a more accurate description. This, however, is rarely simple, for wind currents are fickle at best. But if you are offered the opportunity to figure out the wind — such as in a steady breeze — by all means, use the downwind theory.

Another partial solution — one touted by some, disclaimed by others — is the use of scents — cover-ups and attractants. I use both, but my advice, and I follow it, is to be careful and sparing. In my opinion, moderation is the key.

Cover-ups come in several varieties. These run the gamut from animal scents to various food smells. The claim of some is that the scent will cover the human odor as well as attract deer. Maybe, maybe not.

In the animal scent category, skunk scent has been quite popular, and has seen extensive use over the past years. I have used this, and have seen others use it with success. However, a little goes a long way!

Another animal odor that I have found to be effective is fox urine. This is readily available commercially, and may be a bit less objectionable to the user than is skunk scent.

Scents made from the deer are seen quite often. These, too, have some valid uses. But, and this goes for the use of any scent, be sure that the odor is natural to the time. In the case of other animal or food scents, be sure these are native to the area you are hunting.

For instance, a scent depicting an estrus doe would be out of place if the rut is not in progress. And I have hunted with guys who smelled like a barrel of over-ripe apples. ''Deer like apples,'' they would say. And I'm sure deer do like apples — where these are common. But we were hunting in central Mississippi where the only apples to be found were in the grocery store; and these had been shipped in from hundreds of miles away. I doubt that a Magnolia State whitetail accustomed to acorns, soybeans, and honeysuckle would automatically associate that strange apple scent with a food it is supposed to be crazy about! Use common sense when you use scents.

In my hunting, I use a commercially available fox urine or skunk scent during the early season. When the rut is in progress, a deer-type scent is in order, but I use these very sparingly. I usually put small amounts on scent pads or drag cloths which are left on the ground when I go into my stand. My hope is to draw the deer's attention (sense of smell) away from me and perhaps confound it a bit. I don't want to smell so strongly that the buck, like a high-strung bird dog, points me from 90 yards out.

Stay clean. If possible, shower before you hunt, and use an unscented soap or baking soda. Wear clean clothes that are washed in unscented soap or baking soda and dried outside. I even wrap my camo suit around a bit of vegetation common to my hunting area. This is done several days before the hunt, and the bundle is kept outside away from household odors.

Avoid contact with cooking odors, after shave/deodorants, perfume, gasoline, tobacco, and the like. These are purely human smells, and clothes and hair absorb the odors readily. Get rid of such smells before you head for the deer woods.

Another piece of equipment valuable in the war against smell is a small container to hold your own urine. I consider it as important as my canteen. It is also important not to confuse the two!

A small, plastic bottle is fine, for most hunters can sit throughout a morning or afternoon vigil without expelling urine more than once. A small bottle will hold that. After use, screw a cap securely over the top and set the bottle aside. Carry it out of the woods, or at least away from your hunting area before you empty it.

This process is not meant to get a chuckle or to be disregarded. Indeed, it is a necessity. Give up your cover-ups and attractants before you give up the small bottle to hold your own urine!

Movement is another culprit which must be licked by the bowhunter. Even if you are in a tree stand, sudden movement can alert a deer. It is imperative that you be still. Remaining motionless is a tall order, but if you master it, your success will likely go up.

The time to move and shuffle around is when you first get situated in your tree stand. Spend as much time as is needed to get comfortable. Change angles, make adjustments, organize gear. It is this initial set-up that will greatly determine your long-term comfort, and this will directly affect your ability to sit still.

I have only been caught off guard one time while engaged in this getting-comfortable ritual. I had gotten to my hunting area a bit late, and it was daylight by the time I climbed. All else was settled except my bow. It was about three feet off the ground dangling from a rope. A dandy six-point buck strolled up, checked out the swinging bow, then vanished! It can happen.

Now I realize that it is a rare bowhunter who can for hours on end, sit totally motionless. Indeed, it is a big chore to sit for minutes without movement. I have worked out a system that seems to help me a great deal in this area.

After getting settled and comfortable, I situate my watch so that it can be seen by simply moving my eyes. I set up a block of time — perhaps thirty minutes — and begin a vigil during which I don't move. At the end of that time span, I evaluate things, and determine if I will be able to wait out another similar length of time without moving. If I can, I sit tight. If I feel that some readjustment must be made — maybe I need to use that little bottle I brought along — I plan the movement very carefully.

Before moving, I meticulously check out the area — both with my eyes and ears. I strain to see and/or hear any deer that might have eased into the area. If there is any hint of *Odocoileus virginianus,* I postpone the move. Also, if there has been deer activity during the time I was still, I simply do not move until I know where the deer are — if these critters are still around. If I determine that no deer are in the immediate vicinity, I make my moves, but practically in slow motion. Each move is carefully planned and executed. And while I am moving, I keep my eyes open. There is always a chance that deer are around.

Even with care and planning, the bowhunter will spook deer on occasion. But do your best. Expect a deer at any time.

Chapter 18

TACTICS

EARLY AND LATE SEASON

Depending upon your geographic location, tactics for early and late-season hunting may vary. However, food sources will be a general guideline for choosing your location and carrying out the hunt during these times.

Agricultural crops such as soybeans or corn will likely be drawing cards for early-season deer. The hunter should scout and hunt these while they are being frequented by deer. Refer to the chapter on scouting and location when planning such hunts.

Set up on trails leading to crops. A few yards back into the woods will be preferable. Early mornings and late afternoons will likely be choice for this edge hunting.

Acorns will also be favorite foods during early seasons. Actually, these will remain popular as long as the deer can find them. Keep a watch on hardwood areas. Some fine hunting can be had there.

Browse sign could be a key to locating a concentration of deer. Here, a hunter inspects a heavily used honeysuckle thicket.

Honeysuckle is another natural food that draws deer. Generally, deer seem to work honeysuckle patches more heavily as winter begins to get a grip. If the season framework in your area will allow, check out the honeysuckles late in the year.

I do a majority of my whitetail hunting in the Southeast. Seasons customarily run into late January. It is during this time that green patches get the bowhunter's attention. Rye grass and winter wheat are deer magnets, and if your hunting will allow, keep an eye on such areas. These are hunted in the same manner as the early-season soybean and corn fields. It is not at all unusual to see secluded green patches literally fill with deer as the late afternoon sun drops behind the trees. Don't overlook these.

THE RUT

This annual phenomenon is perhaps the very best time during which to arrow a good buck. The animals are on the move, and bucks tend to lose a bit of their caution. The time of the rut varies greatly with geographic regions.

Scrapes — those shallow, pawed-out depressions — are the most obvious indications that the rut is underway. And though scrapes are not fully understood, we do know that bucks make the scrapes, and that these bucks will check primary scrapes regularly. If you happen to be there when one of the critters makes his round, you could put venison in the freezer and a trophy on the wall.

Look for scrapes along logging roads, ridge tops, and field edges. After locating a series of scrapes, watch them and try to determine if these are active and being worked regularly. If so, this could be a hot-spot. If scrapes are not being freshened, these are likely secondary or incidental scrapes, and may be only marginally productive.

This hunter is preparing to set up along a fresh scrape line. The trail of scrapes was along the side of a ridge that dropped off into a small drainage.

When you find active scrapes in an area, get ready to spend some time there. You will need to incorporate all you have learned about scouting, stand location, scents, and movement to collect your buck, but he is present, and you have a good chance of seeing him along that active scrape line.

Set up downwind. Get no closer to the scrapes than is required for a good shot. Don't follow the buck's trail when going to your stand. Keep disturbance to a minimum. Be particularly careful regarding scent and movement. And spend some hours in your stand. While early mornings and late afternoons remain peak times, a rutting buck may show up at any time. Be persistent. When you bring down a rutting buck by using your archery tackle, the rewards will be far greater than the effort required to take him.

Chapter 19

PICK A SPOT

Shoot at a specific spot on the deer and not just at the deer. This often-heard advice could easily be the most important and most overlooked when the bowhunter finds himself in those critical few seconds during a hunting situation. The entire hunt can easily hinge on the shooter's calm approach to blocking out all else and concentrating on a spot that will place the arrow into the vitals. The penalty for a shot anywhere else is usually rather severe.

Now don't think that this failure to concentrate and pick a spot on the animal happens only to newcomers to bowhunting. Indeed, veterans fall prey to this sneaky villain occasionally. I have a tendency to fling an arrow over a deer's back from time to time, and this is due to not finding that spot and settling the sight pin.

One of my favorite hunting companions is an outstanding bowhunter. He has taken many whitetails, mule deer, and elk. This past season he was the victim of a bad case of buck fever (or elk fever) while bowhunting elk in Colorado. He had bugled in a dandy five-point bull, and the big critter offered a broadside shot at fifteen steps. "I just drew the bow and shot, " he told me. "I broke that all-important rule of picking a spot. You would have thought that I was a complete novice." The arrow zipped harmlessly under the out-sized bull.

There is no magic spot to choose when settling in for a shot. My favorite is just behind the shoulder about half-way down from the top of the deer's back. This requires a broadside or slightly quartering-away position to properly execute. Such a shot will generally strike the lungs — my preferred target.

The heart shot is also good, but the target is quite small. For this, hold rather low on the chest cavity just behind the front leg. I really don't like this — even though it is most lethal — so I opt for the lung shot.

When shooting from a tree stand, it is entirely possible to have a deer under you. When such a shot presents itself, I put the pin between the shoulder blades. The chances of clipping the spine with such a shot are very good. If this is done, the deer will pile up. If the arrow misses the spine, it will — assuming the broadhead is razor sharp, and is being propelled by adequate force — procede through vitals such as lungs and heart. Hopefully, the broadhead will punch through on the bottom side. An animal thus hit will surely go down, and there should be a strong blood trail leading to the deer.

Without question there are other shots/positions that will bring a deer down. However, most are risky, and more difficult to make. Personally, I choose to pass unless I get the straight-down or lung shot I look for. I would encourage other bowhunters, particularly beginners, to do the same. Letting a deer walk away without taking a shot may sound strange and unreasonable; but think about it. The deer, a fantastic and majestic game animal, gives the hunter its best. Should you, the hunter, do less?

A chart showing the deer's vitals can be a big aid when preparing for a bowhunt. Study it, and know where those vulnerable areas are. Also, practice on a life-size deer target, and

Know where the vitals are located and place your arrow accordingly. Charts and targets showing these vital areas will be helpful.

get accustomed to shooting for the vitals and not just at the deer. Pick a spot that will take the arrow to the boiler room, and settle the pin there. Forget the other aspects of the deer. Concentrate, release smoothly, and you should, within minutes, enjoy the fruit of your labor.

PART VIII

After the Shot

Follow a hit deer carefully. Take care to stay on the trail and be careful that you don't cover the sign that is left.

Chapter 20

TRACKING

If you have done things right up to this point, a downed deer will be your reward. But, even with a well-placed arrow, some tracking will probably be required. However, this should be only a small chore, and is certainly nothing to dread.

At the shot the deer will likely run. The exception to this will be a deer that has sustained a broken neck, spine, or has been hit in the brain by the arrow. Such an animal will usually drop and never regain its footing. If the deer runs off, watch it carefully. Also, listen intently. Many times the bowhunter will hear the deer fall and thrash around before succumbing to its wound. Generally, the archer can then walk straight to the deer.

Although it is difficult to do, it is important for the bowhunter to give the deer a few minutes before following. Arguments arise regarding how long to wait. In my opinion, the time span will depend upon the hit. If you see that arrow punch through the lung/heart area, the deer is down, and probably only a short distance out. However, if you suspect a poor hit, an hour wait is probably in order.

When a well-hit deer runs after the shot, I sit on my stand, calm down a bit, and collect my thoughts and gear. I may spend fifteen minutes there. After that, I descend the tree quietly. If the deer is down permanently, there is no need to rush. If not, I want to make as little noise as is necessary in an effort to avoid spooking the deer — which is probably lying down.

I go to the spot where the deer was standing when I shot and look for the arrow. This should help me determine whether or not I made a hit if there is any question regarding such. Hair and/or blood will likely show up within a few yards. I follow the trail left by the deer and immediately begin a stalk just as if I were hunting. Remember, it is important not to jump the deer if it is still alive.

While stalking the sign, keep an eye out ahead. Stop every few feet and search the area around you. Take it easy. If you see the deer stretched out with no signs of life, approach cautiously with an arrow ready. If you detect that the deer is still alive, freeze. Hopefully, the animal will not leave that spot before the arrow does its job.

If you happen to get within shooting range of a deer that is down but not out, there is some debate whether or not to shoot. An arrow at this point could spook the deer into a headlong dash that might lead to an extensive trailing job. Use your own discretion. If I had a good shot, and felt that I could place an arrow into a vital zone, I would opt to send a shaft on its way. If the chances of a good hit are slim, it is probably best to wait.

Another reason for stalking and moving slowly on trail is to accurately follow that trail. It is entirely possible for a fatally wounded deer to leave very little or no blood. This is the case when an arrow enters high and doesn't exit. In such a situation, the bowhunter must trail without the aid of blood.

Tracks are the most obvious. A hit deer may stumble, drag a foot, or otherwise disturb the ground — this is particularly evident in leaves — more than usual. Take care to follow such sign, and be especially careful not to disrupt it. Walk off to one side so that the sign left by the deer will remain.

Broken twigs or crushed grass may also be along the deer's path. It may become necessary to get on hands and knees to follow. If you lose the trail, mark the spot where you found the last sign. This will give a reference point from which to begin your search for more sign. A handerkerchief or tissue paper works fine for marking sign. I prefer orange flagging, and keep a small roll with me at all times.

Even though it is a less than desirable situation, after dark tracking may become a necessity. If so, don't panic. Equip yourself and get at it.

Flashlights are good for following a trail after dark, but nothing beats a lantern — the Coleman lantern is excellent. These units throw a broad area of light rather than a single spot, and a blood trail practically leaps out at you in the glow of such lanterns. Keep one in your vehicle or at camp. It could spell the difference between a recovered or lost deer. Also, check the laws governing this practice in your area.

There are tracking devices on the market today that are designed to lay a trail of string from a spool attached to the bow to the deer via the arrow. The concept is somewhat sound, but I have not had any experience with these. You may choose to check this out.

Chapter 21

PROPER FIELD CARE

To help assure high-quality venison, proper field care is mandatory. The animal should be field-dressed immediately, then chilled as quickly as possible. In warm weather, this may require getting the carcass to a packing plant. I have quartered deer and put the parts in neighbor's refrigerators on many occasions. This will allow time to properly process the meat.

For the uninitiated, field-dressing must seem a real chore. Actually, it is not, and can be accomplished quickly. A sharp knife is all that will be needed.

Basic field-dressing consists of getting the internal organs out of the deer. This is best accomplished by rolling the deer onto its back. Stand behind or a-straddle the deer, and spread the back legs apart. Begin the incision at the back of the abdominal cavity and work forward up into the sternum. Take care to cut only the hide and muscle/membrane surrounding the entrails.

After the deer is opened, reach as far up into the chest cavity as possible and sever the esophagus/windpipe. This frees the organs up near the neck. Work around the dia-

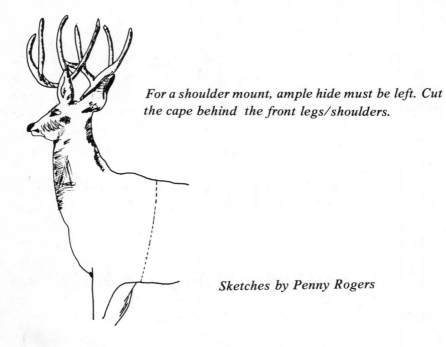

For a shoulder mount, ample hide must be left. Cut the cape behind the front legs/shoulders.

Sketches by Penny Rogers

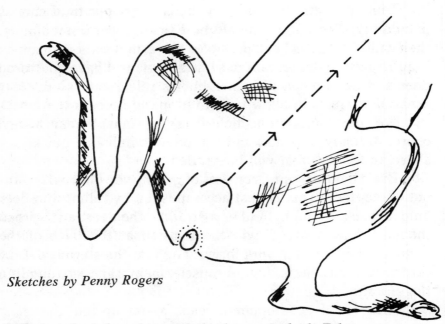

Sketches by Penny Rogers

Field-dressing is best done with the deer on its back. Take care to cut only the hide and membrane surrounding the insides.

phragm and membranes that hold the organs at the rib cage area. Be sure that all are cut or pulled free. Ring the anus from the outside (and vulva on a doe) to free the intestine. This can then be pulled from the inside. Roll the deer onto its side and the viscera will spill out. Drag the deer away from the remains and place the carcass with the opening slanted downward. This will allow it to drain.

During the field-dressing chore, take care not to cut or puncture the internal organs, including the bladder. Do your best to get these out intact. If you do cut an organ and its contents get on the meat, use whatever is available to clean it off. Leaves, dry cloths, or perhaps a bit of creek water will help. Failure to do so could result in tainted, strong-tasting venison.

The hide helps to protect the meat while a deer is being dragged from the woods or otherwise transported. However, to facilitate cooling, it should be removed as quickly as possible. If it is necessary to leave the hide on for any length of time, hang the deer and prop the body cavity open with a stick. If at all possible, I get the hide off and the carcass hung in a cool place within a couple of hours of my hunt.

If flies are a problem, and this could easily be the case, a mesh game bag may be in order. These allow air to circulate around the meat, but help keep unwanted pollutants from the meat. These bags are particularly useful if a deer must hang in camp overnight.

Field care for the venison is not the only consideration of the bowhunter. If he bags a trophy — and all deer taken with a bow are trophies — he may want a mount. This requires care.

My taxidermist friend says that the most often-made mistake regarding a potential mount is cutting the cape too short. A shoulder mount requires plenty of hide, and the hunter should cut the cape on a line that runs behind the front legs. This will give the taxidermist adequate hide with which to work.

Also, take care not to cut through the hide in any area that will be used in the mount. This usually occurs in the skinning

A properly wrapped cape will keep for some time in the freezer.
Even so, get it to the taxidermist as soon as possible.

process, but can be avoided if the hunter takes his time.

Keep the cape clean. Avoid letting it come in contact with blood, petroleum products, or the like. Such things can stain and mat the hair.

The best thing to do with a head that is to be mounted is to get it to the taxidermist immediately. If this is not possible, wrap it securely — garbage bags are fine — and freeze it. Even so, don't forget about it and leave it frozen for long periods. It can freezer burn. Turn it over to the taxidermist soon.

You are about to begin a hunting experience like no other. Bowhunting. It is fantastic!

Choose equipment carefully; practice long; exercise respect for the land-owner, your fellow hunter, and the game you seek; work hard; be persistent; and enjoy!

INDEX

Books available through Survival Medical Outfitters, P.O. Box 10102, Merrillville, Indiana 46410. Check, money order, VISA, and Mastercard accepted; please include expiration date of card. Write or call (219) 769-0585.

Commercial orders must be addressed to Stackpole Books, P.O. Box 1831, Cameron and Kelker Streets, Harrisburg, Pennsylvania 17105. For fast service use the toll free number. Call 1-800-READ NOW. For library telemarketing orders, call 1-800-LIBRARI. In Pennsylvania, call (717) 234-5041. Please call between 8:30 a.m. and 4:00 p.m. EST.

WILDERNESS MEDICINE
William W. Forgey, M.D.
An informative medical procedures manual written specifically for outdoorsmen interested in preventing, diagnosing and treating common illnesses and injuries. Emergency medical and surgical techniques are described in simple terms. Devoted to the selection of medications, both prescription and non-prescription and their use under wilderness conditions. **Paperback**, 5½ x 8½, 120 pages, photos, diagrams, illus. 0-934802-14-9 **$9.95** Canadian $12.95

"... a clear, concise guide to treating the gamut of outdoor mishaps, from insect bites and fishhook removal to more serious problems such as broken bones and heatstroke."
Sports Afield 11/84

HYPOTHERMIA - Death by Exposure
by William W. Forgey, M.D.
Hypothermia is the lowering of the body's core temperature to the point that illness and death can result. It can be prevented. It can be treated. But only if you know how. Hypothermia is the greatest potential danger for anyone traveling in the outdoors -- whether fishing, hunting, camping, climbing, or even driving down an Interstate Highway. Outdoors medical expert, Dr. William Forgey, explores the causes, methods of prevention, advances in clothing, field treatments, hospital care, and the basics of physiology and physics of hypothermia in terms everyone can understand. Paperback, , 6x9, 172 pages, illus., index, glossary, bibliography.
ISBN 0-934802-10-6 **$9.95** Canadian $12.95

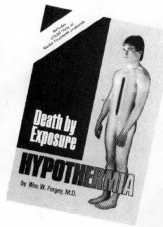

CANOEING WILD RIVERS
Cliff Jacobson
An easy reading manual, of source material, canoeing tips, advanced techniques, and gear recommendations by a weathered expert. **Paperback**, 340 pages, color photos, illus.
0-934802-17-3 **$14.95** Canadian 17.95

"If you've ever dreamed of canoeing Alaska's arctic rivers, or for that matter, any waterway in North America, then Canoeing Wild Rivers is the first book you should obtain."
Alaska Outoors 11/84

"This book, Canoeing Wild Rivers, by Cliff Jacobson is the one I recommend above all others ... It is not a re-hash of previous writers, but the accumulated learnings of much personal experience."
Verlen Kruger ['84]
Ultimate Canoe Challenge member

HIKING
Calvin Rutstrum
A comprehensive, procedural coverage from the short urban walk to the extensive wilderness trek, with analysis of equipment, outdoor living methods, and modern hiking ethics. **Paperback**, 6x9, 125 pages, photos, illus.
0-934802-20-3 **$8.95** Canadian $11.95

BACK COUNTRY
Calvin Rutstrum
A volume of adventures, trips and events from the Northern Wilderness during the first part of this century. **Paperback**, 6x9, 255 pages, Les Kouba illus.
0-934802-11-4 **$14.95** Canadian $17.95

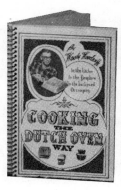

COOKING THE DUTCH OVEN WAY
Woody Woodruff

Written by a designer/manufacturer of dutch ovens, and a 50-year Scouter and life-long camper and hiker. Recipes for good old fashioned dishes and baker's favorites, easily prepared at home or in the northwoods. **Paperback**, 6x9, 142 pages, illus. 0-934802-01-7 **$8.95** Canadian $11.95

A TRAPPER'S LEGACY
Carl Schels

A rare glimpse of a professional trapper's life, difficulties, and dangers of existence deep in the wilderness. Forced into poverty by the Great Depression, Carl Schels decided to chase his dream of wilderness living and survived to write this story -- his legacy. **Paperback**, 5½ x 8½, 212 pages, photos. 0-934802-12-2 **$9.95** Canadian $12.95

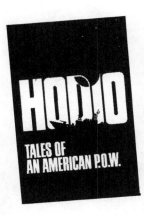

HODIO
C.N. Day

The true story of a 19-year-old American seaman captured off the shores of Burma during a naval battle of World War II. For the 42 months in brutal prison camps of Indonesia, **HODIO** became synonymous with Prisoner of War. **Paperback**, 5½ x 8½, 216 pages. 0-934802-13-0 **$9.95** Canadian $12.95